Be
Mine

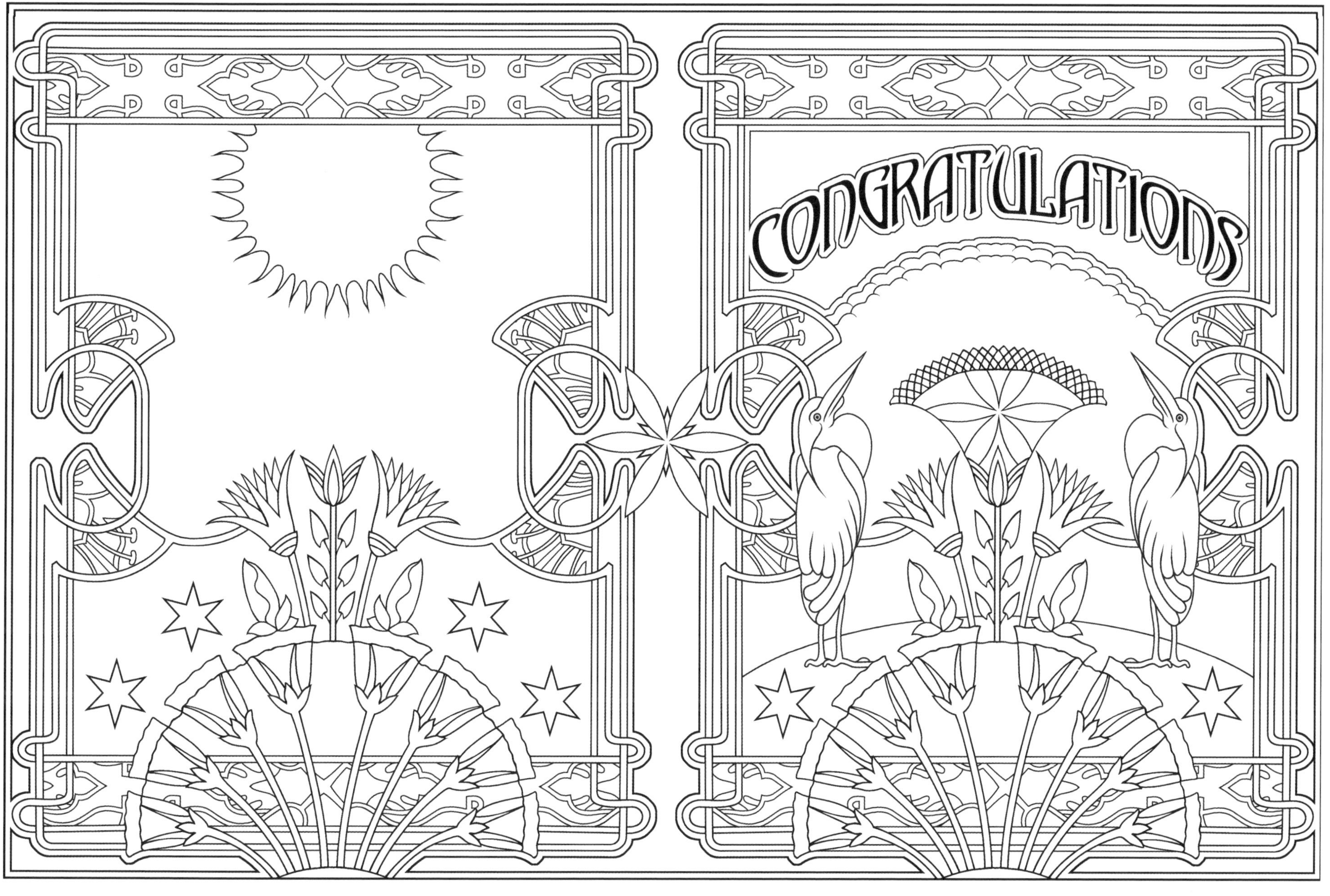
CONGRATULATIONS

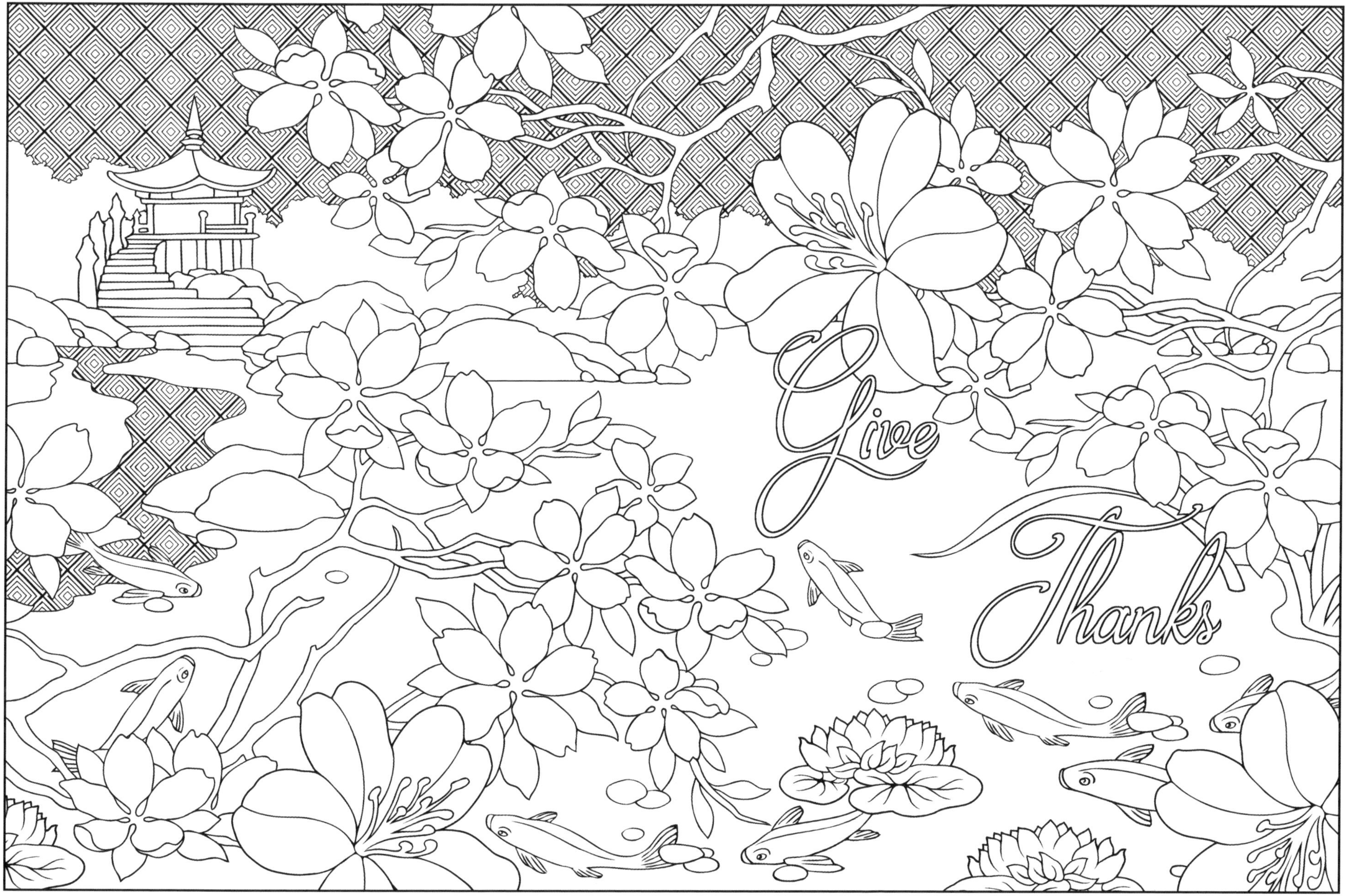
Give
Thanks

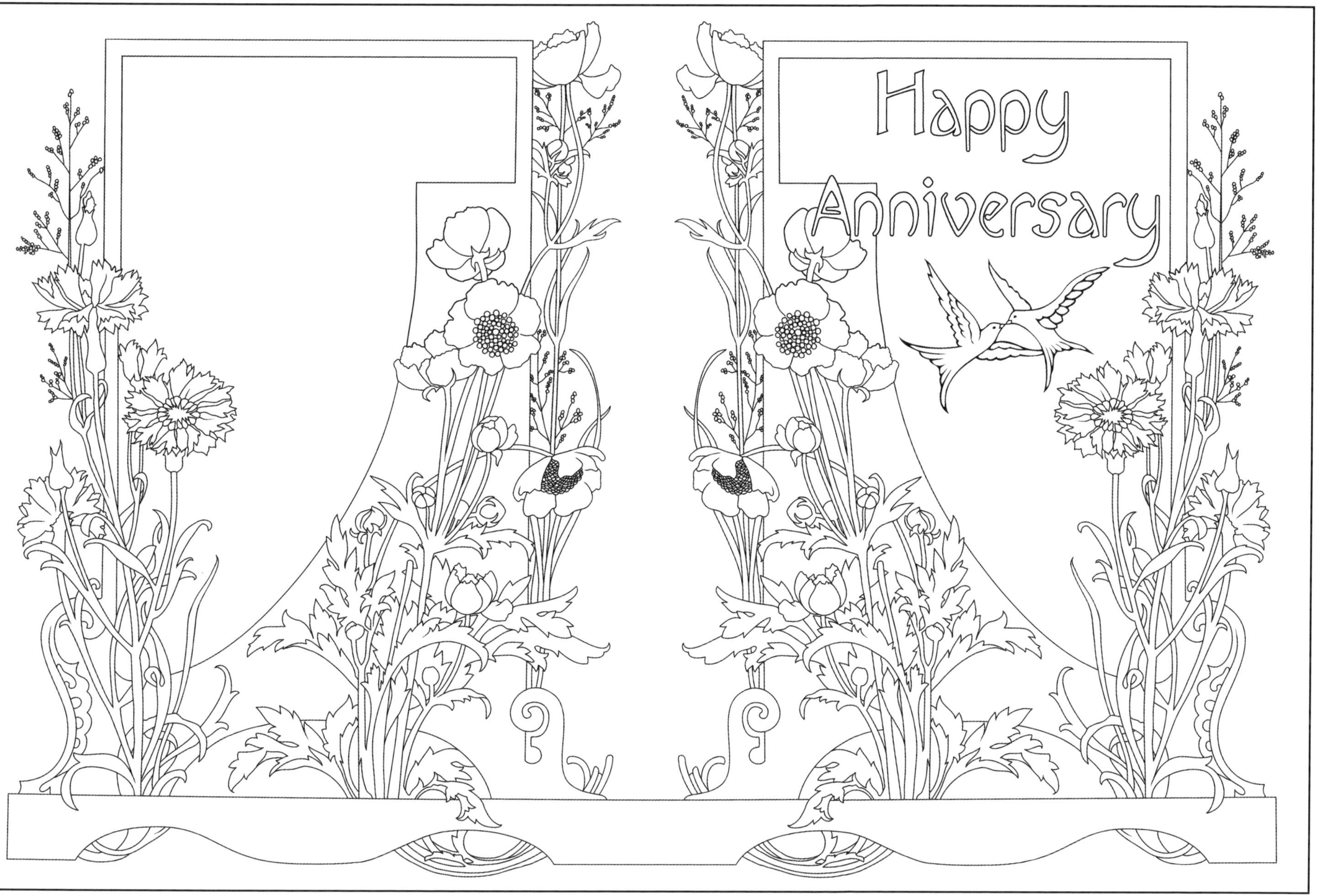
Happy
Anniversary

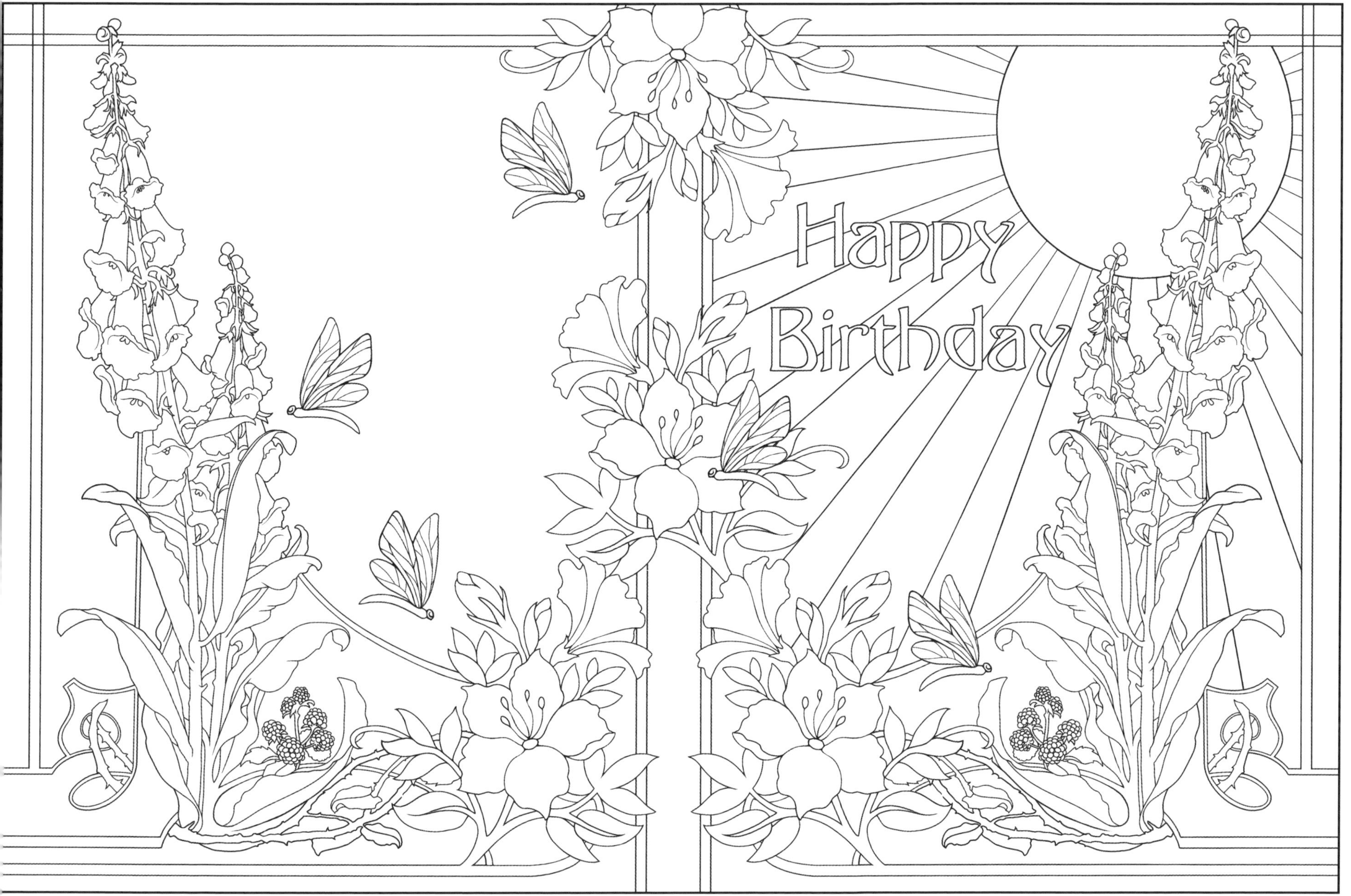
Happy
Birthday

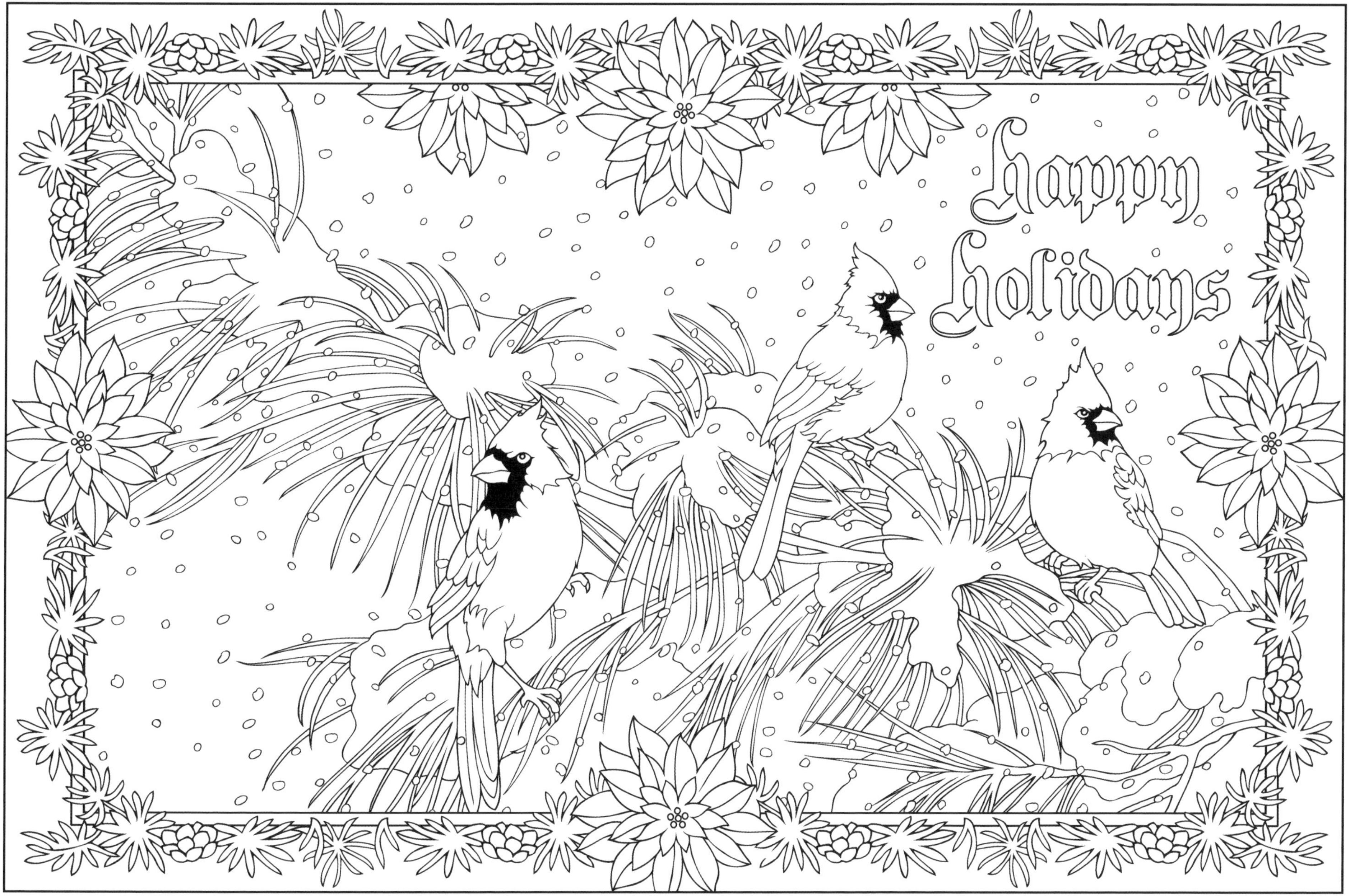
Happy
Holidays

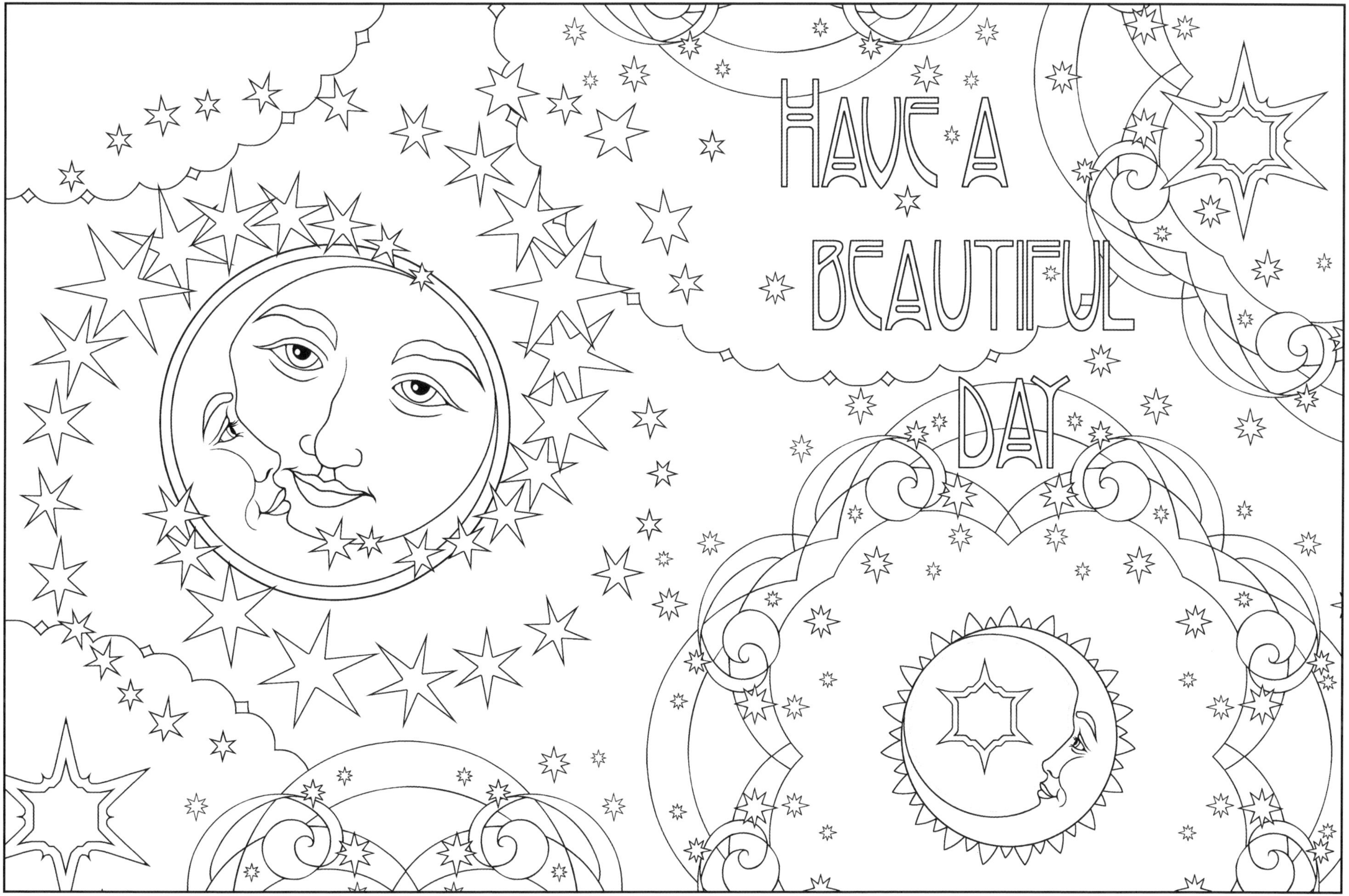
HAVE A
BEAUTIFUL
DAY

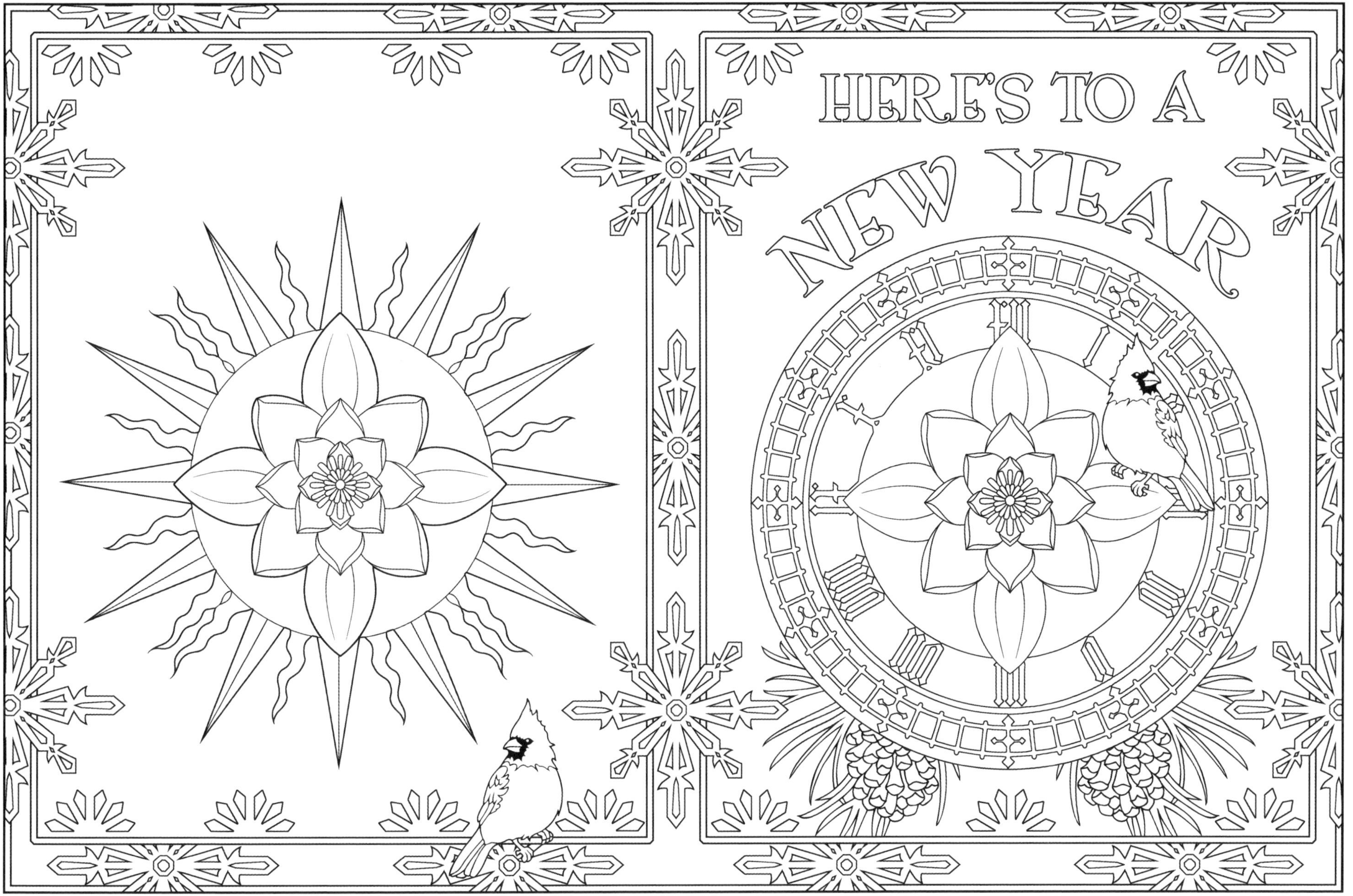
HERE'S TO A
NEW YEAR

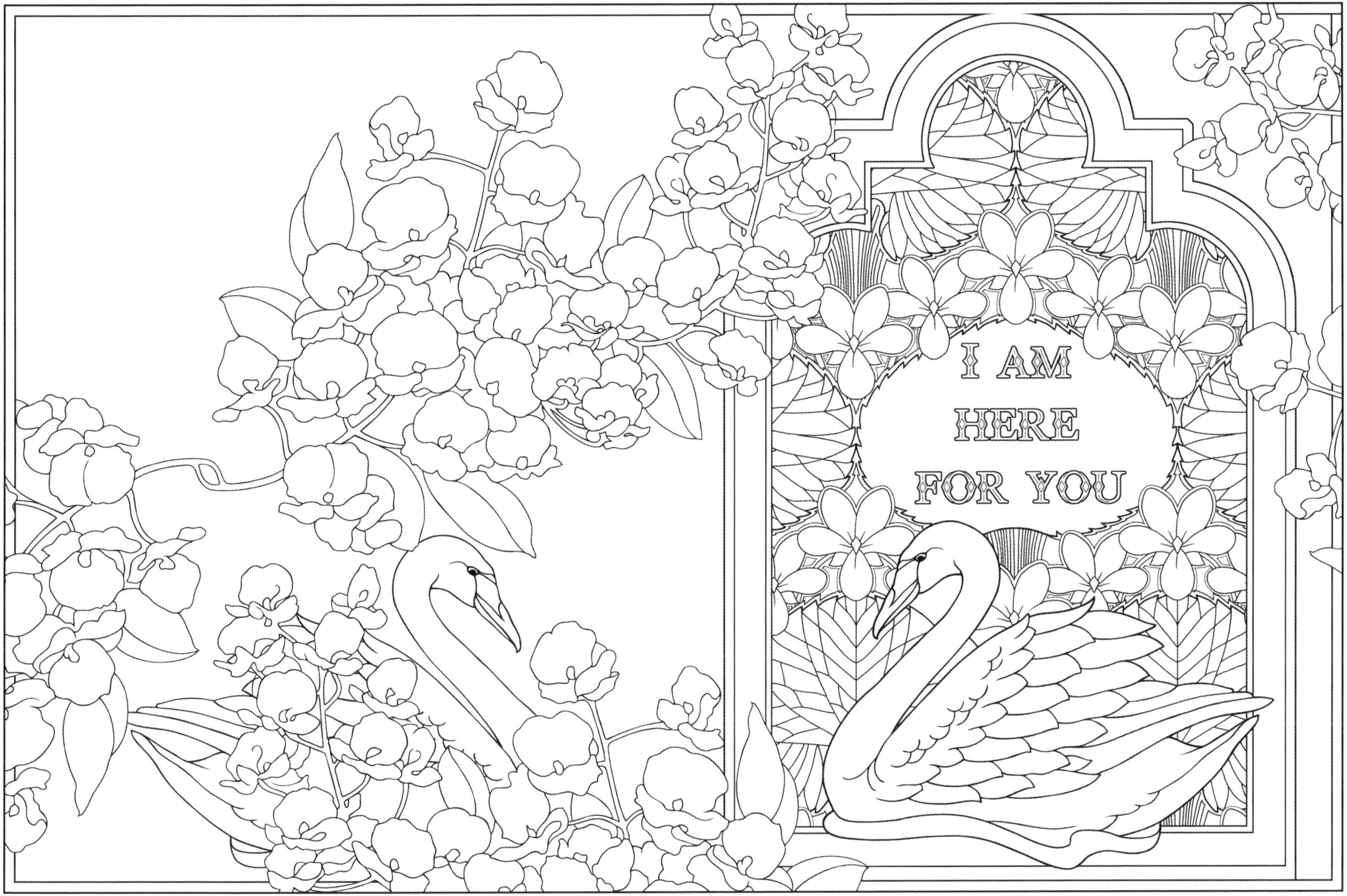
I AM
HERE
FOR YOU

I
LOVE
YOU

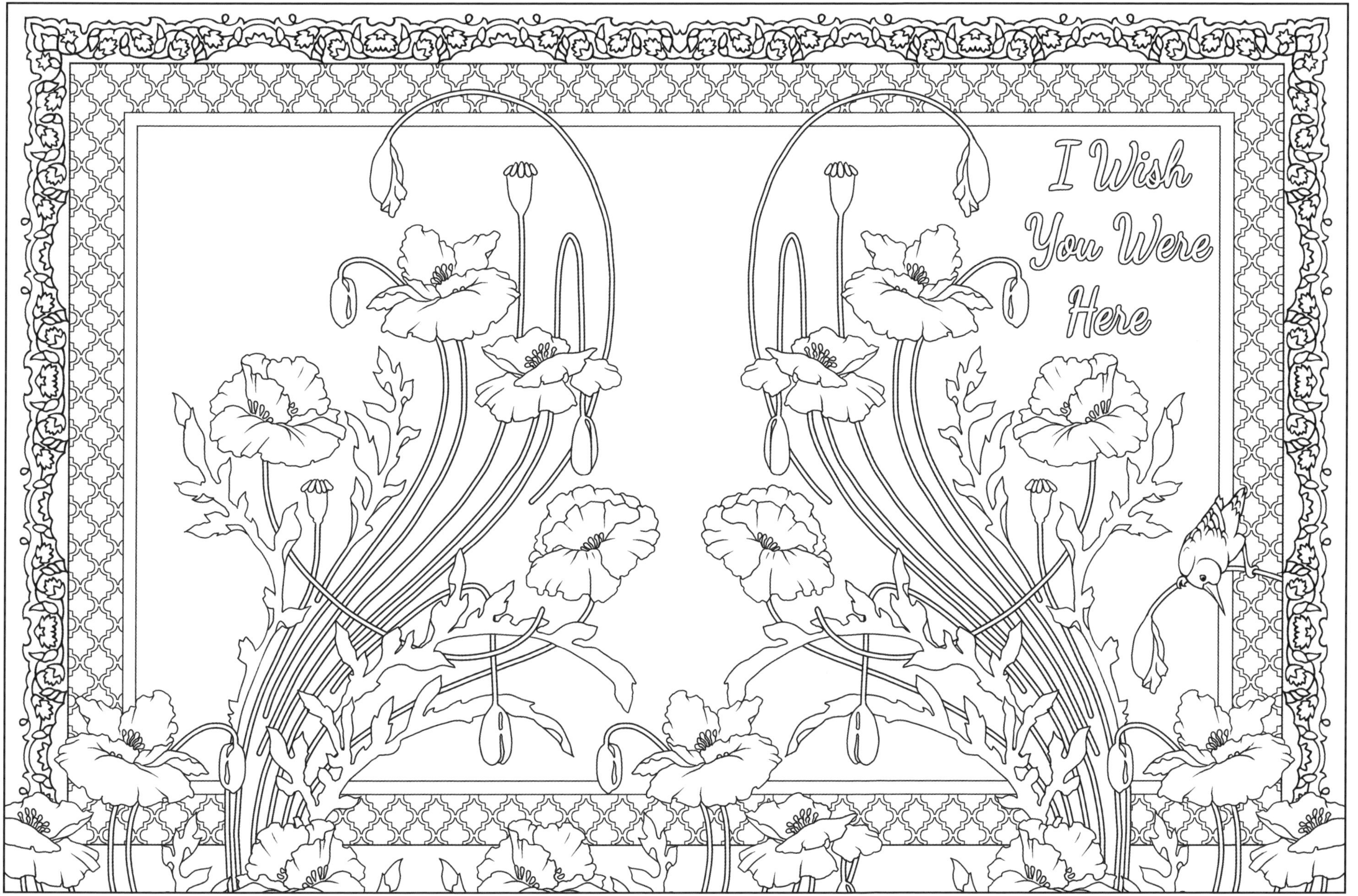
I Wish
You Were
Here

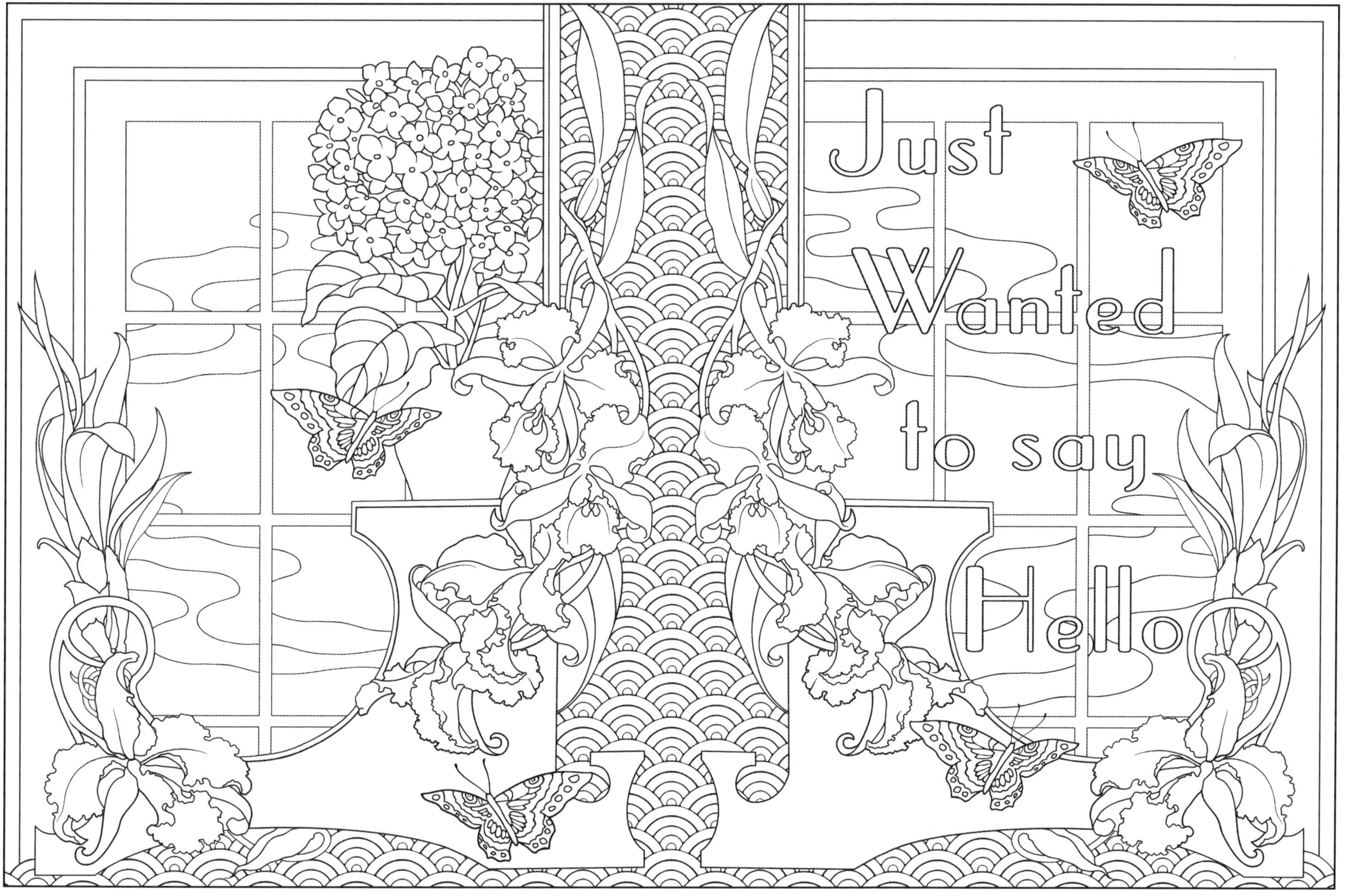
Just
Wanted
to say
Hello

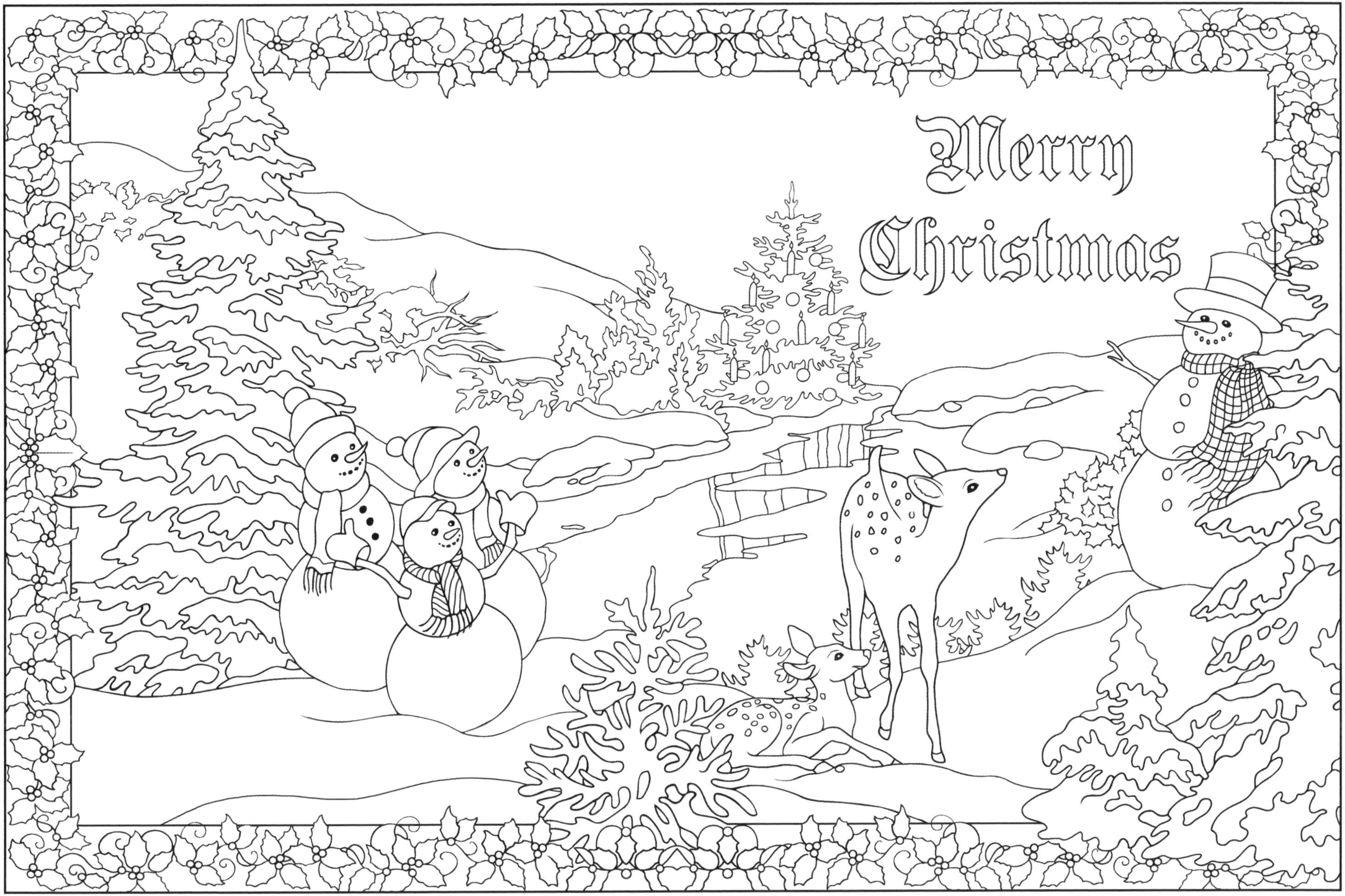
Merry
Christmas

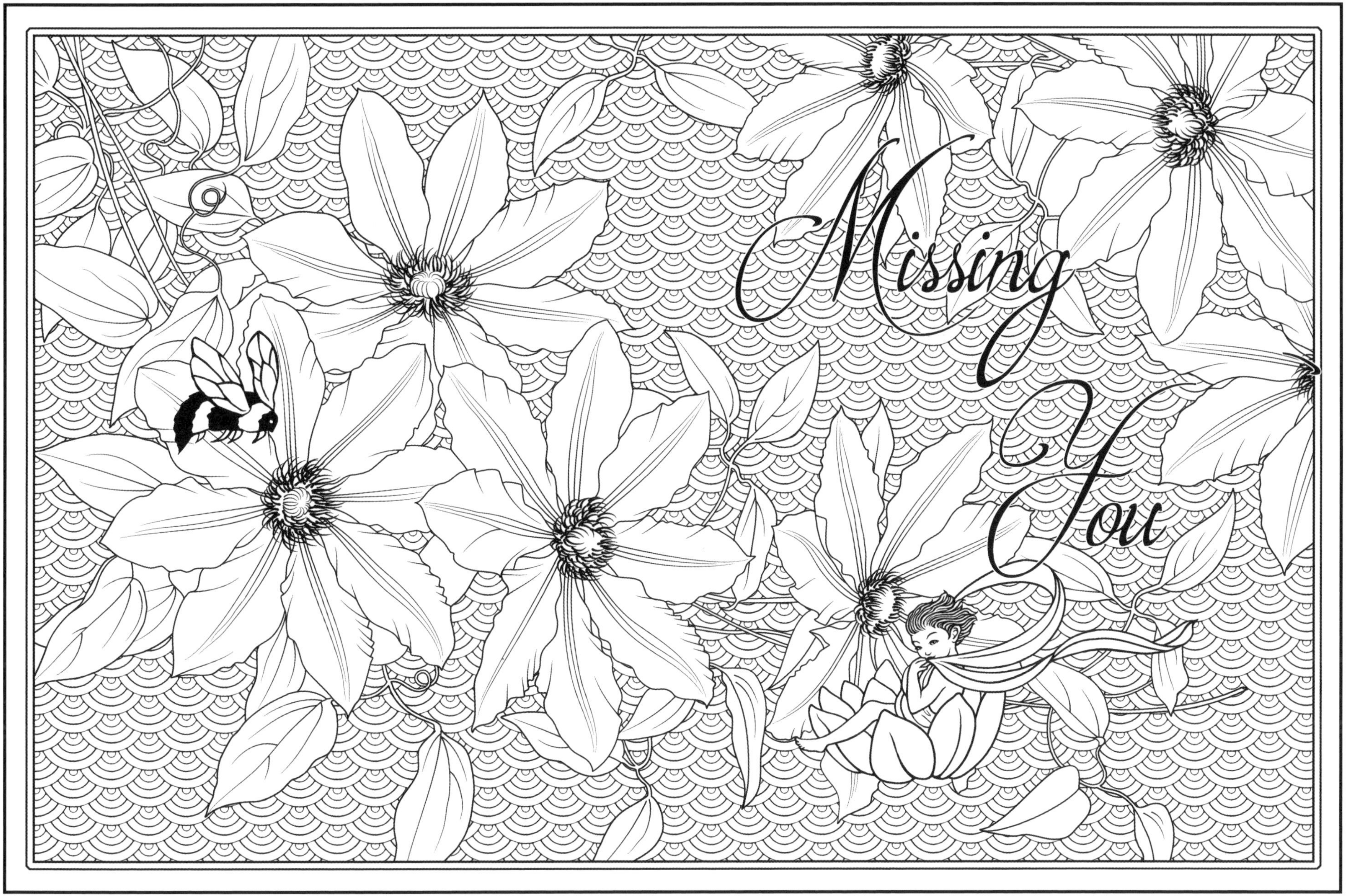
Missing You

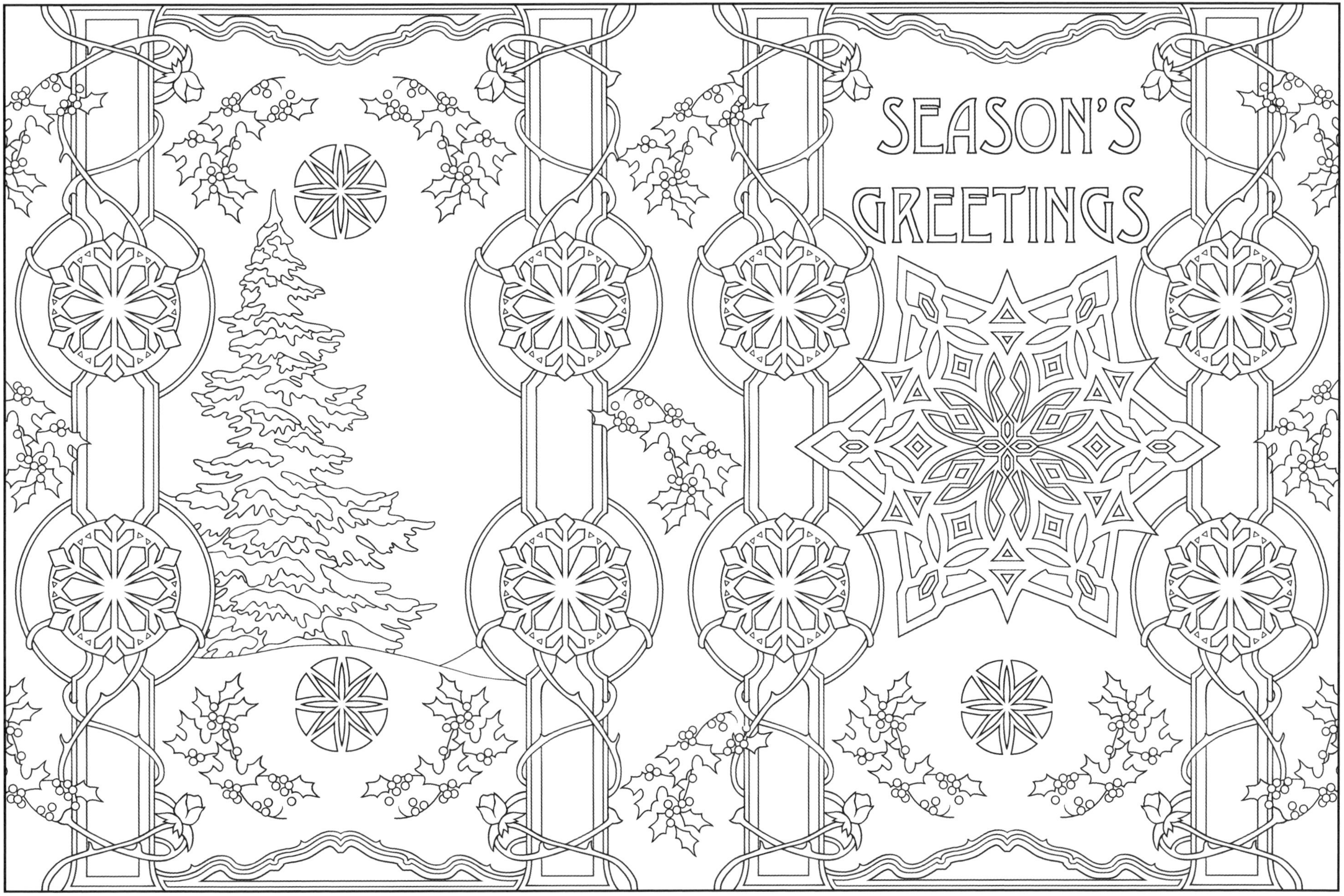
SEASON'S
GREETINGS

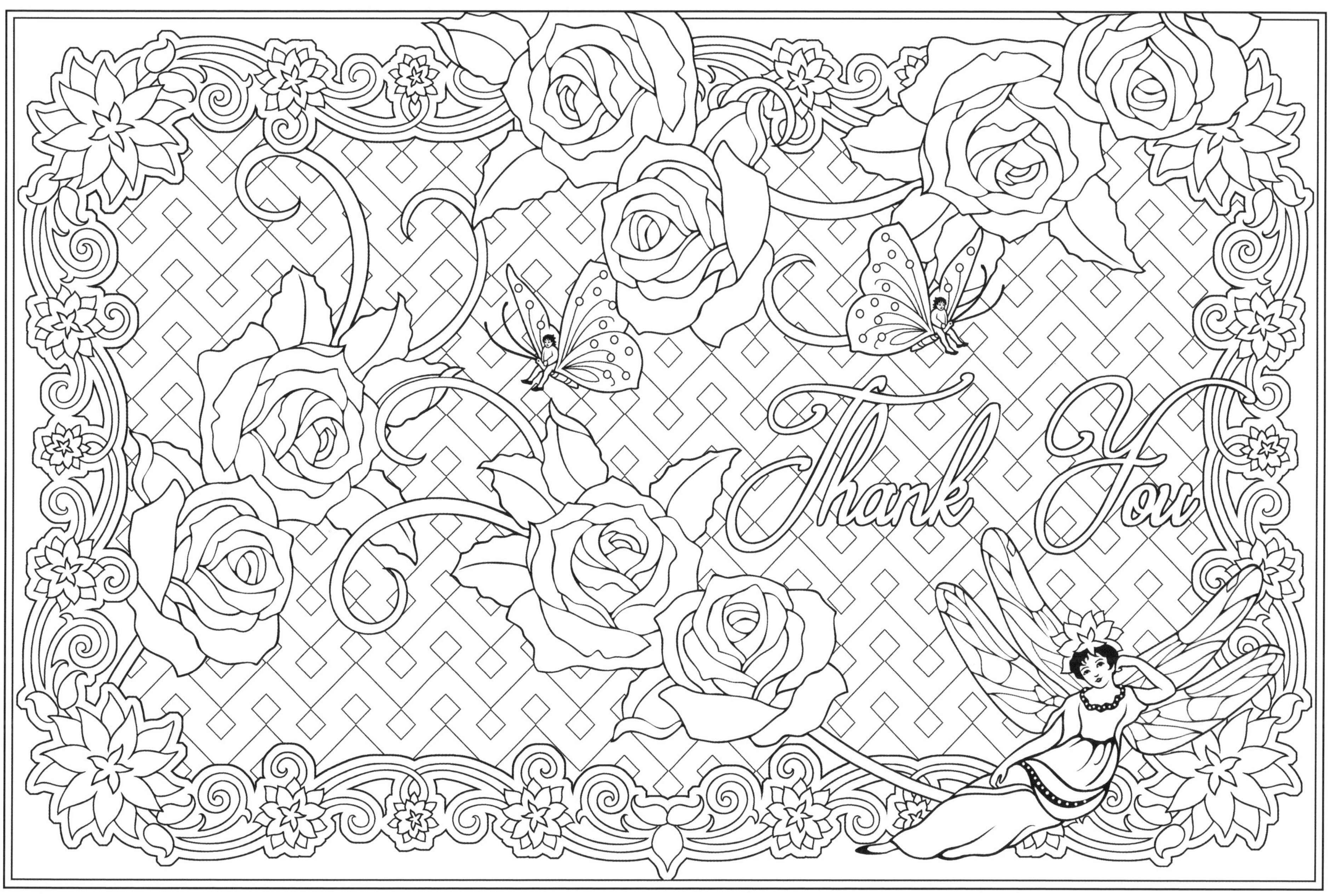
Thank You

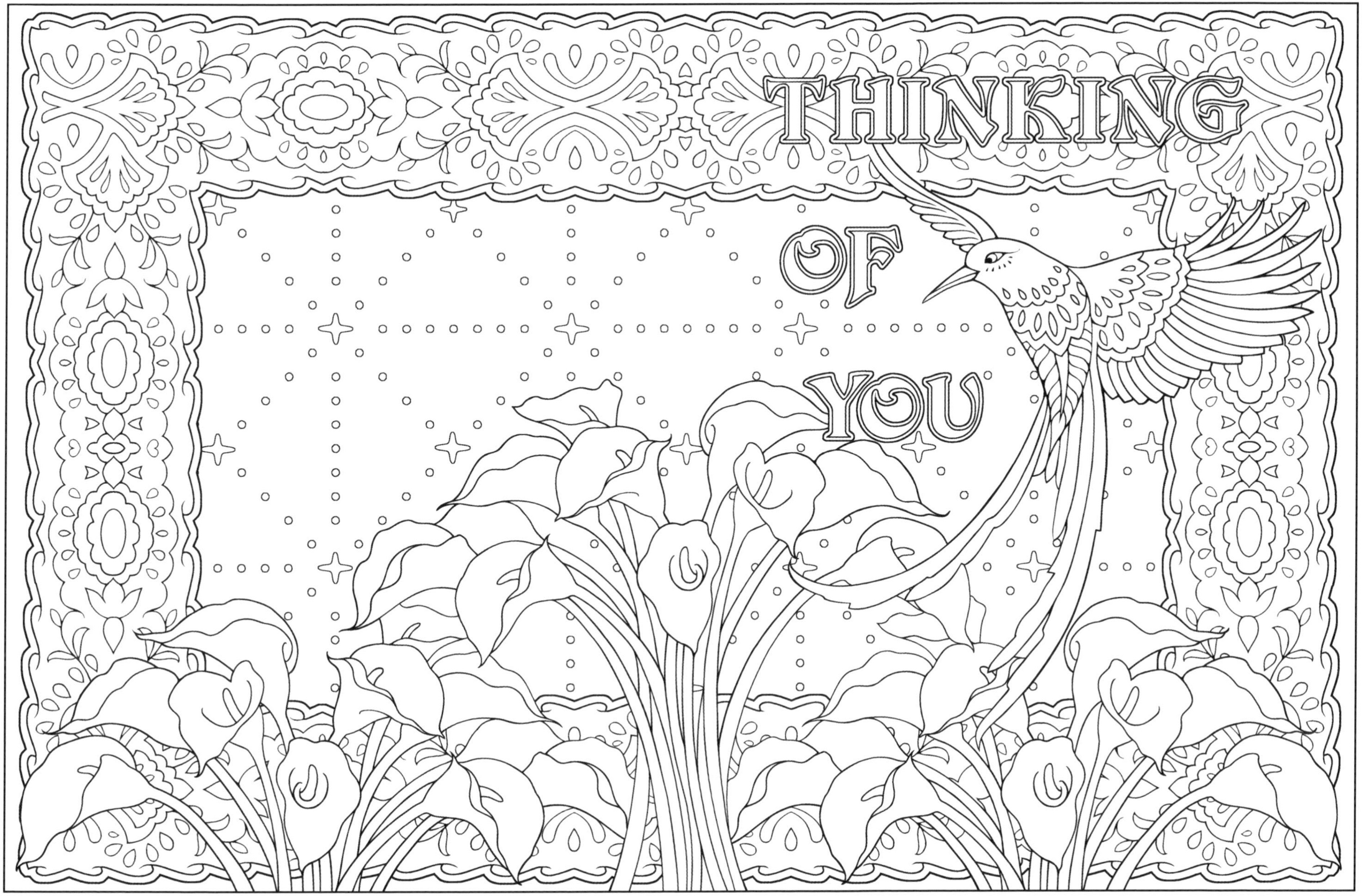
THINKING
OF
YOU

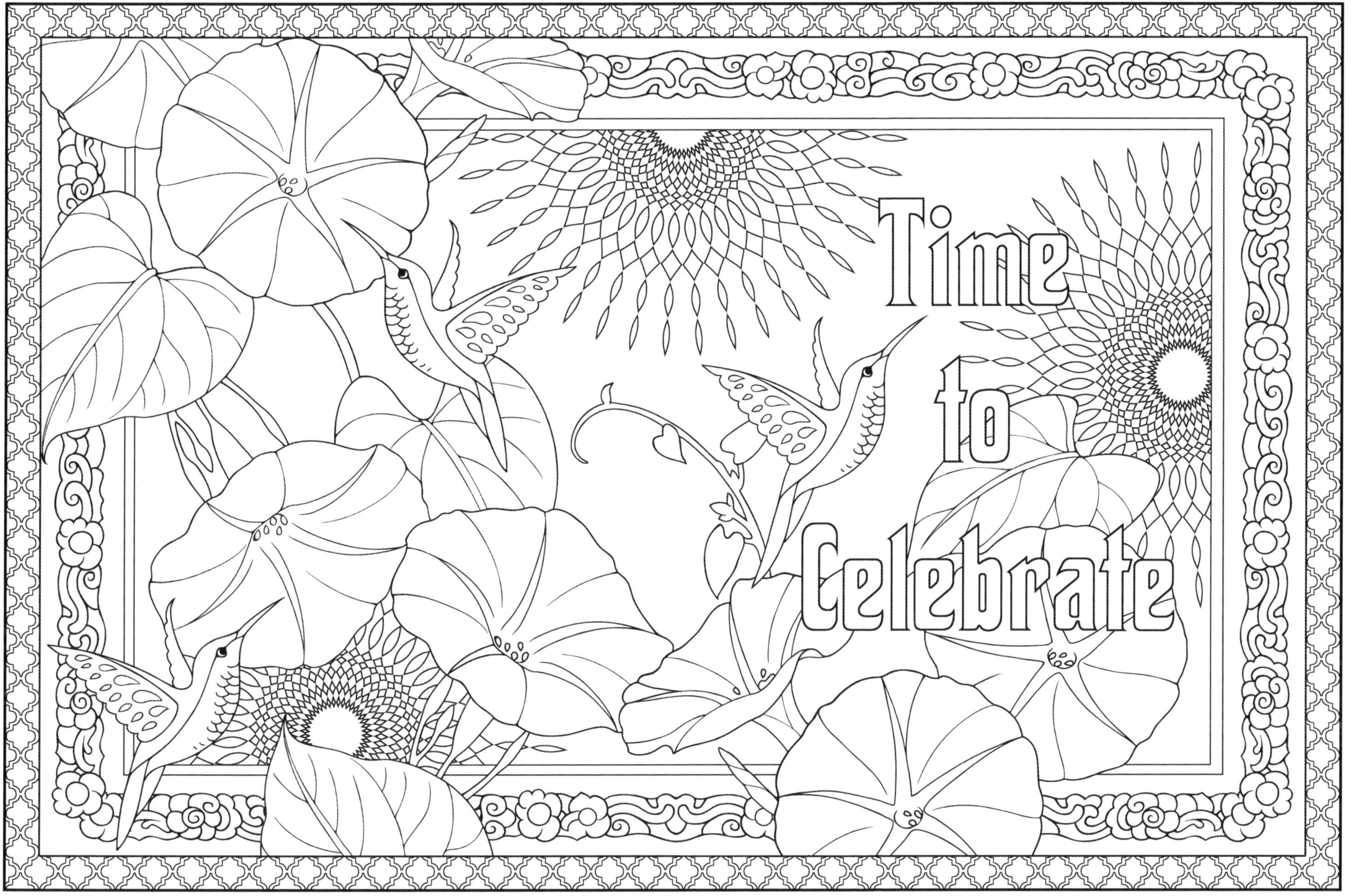
Time
to
Celebrate

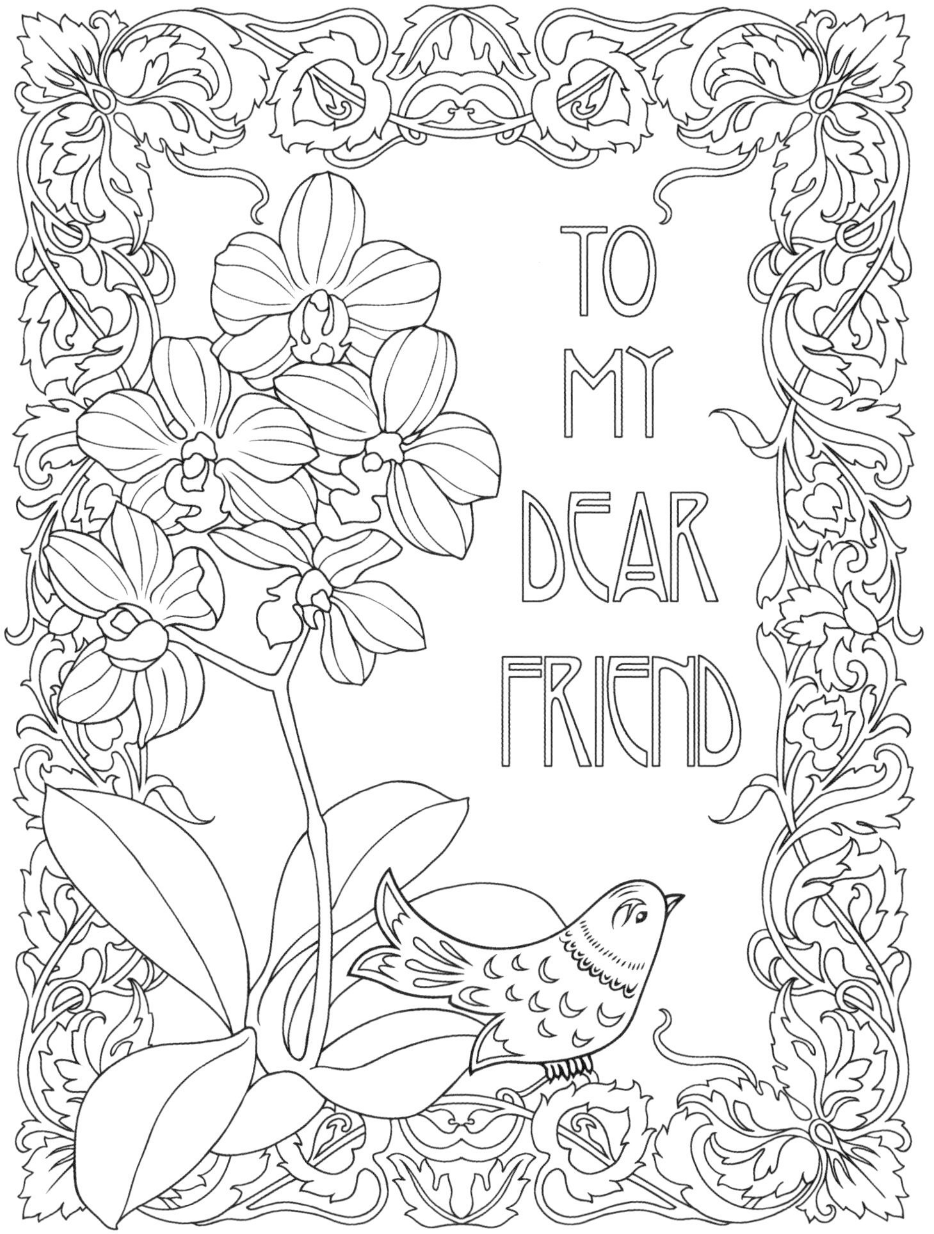
TO
MY
DEAR
FRIEND

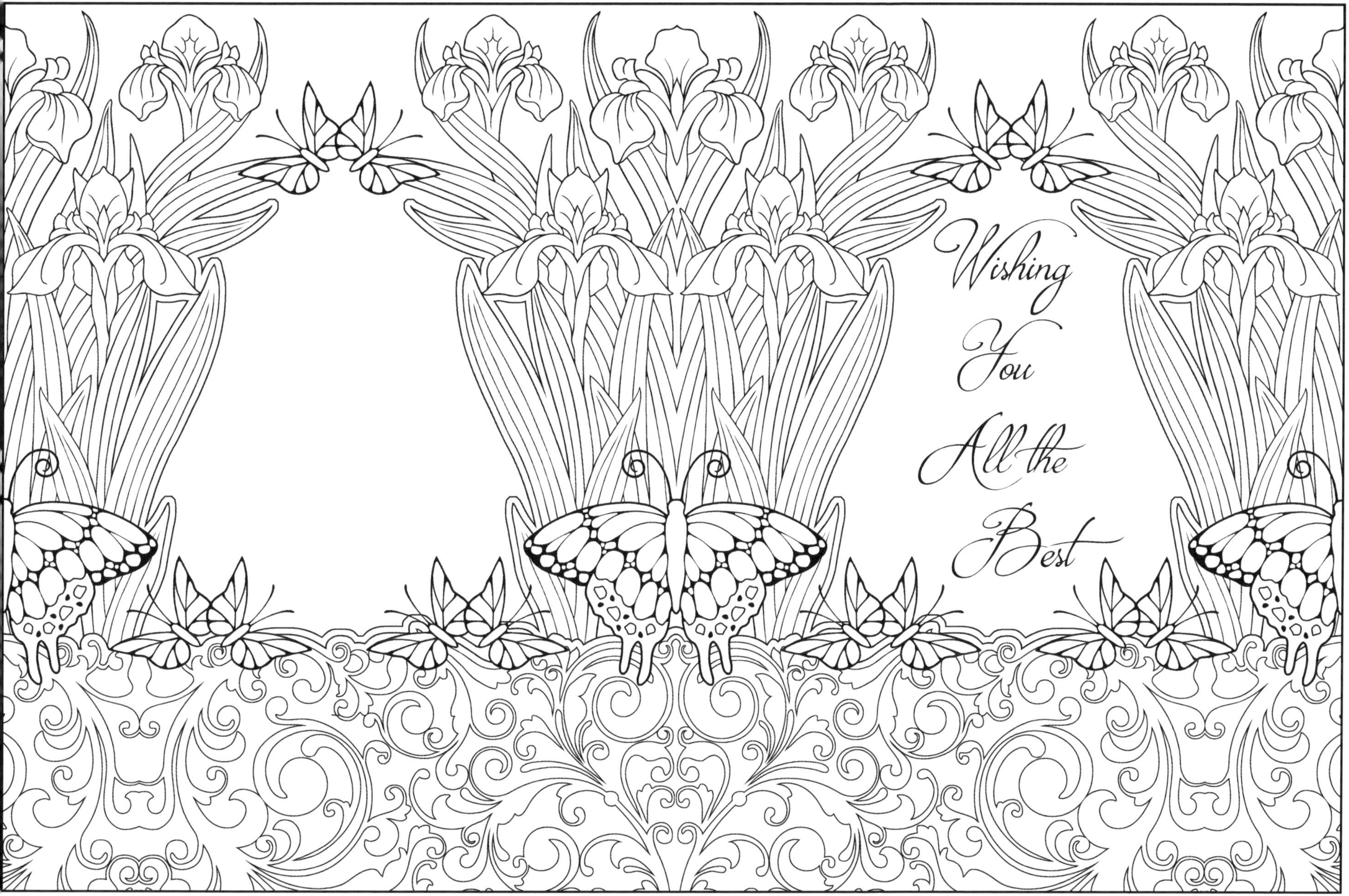
Wishing You All the Best

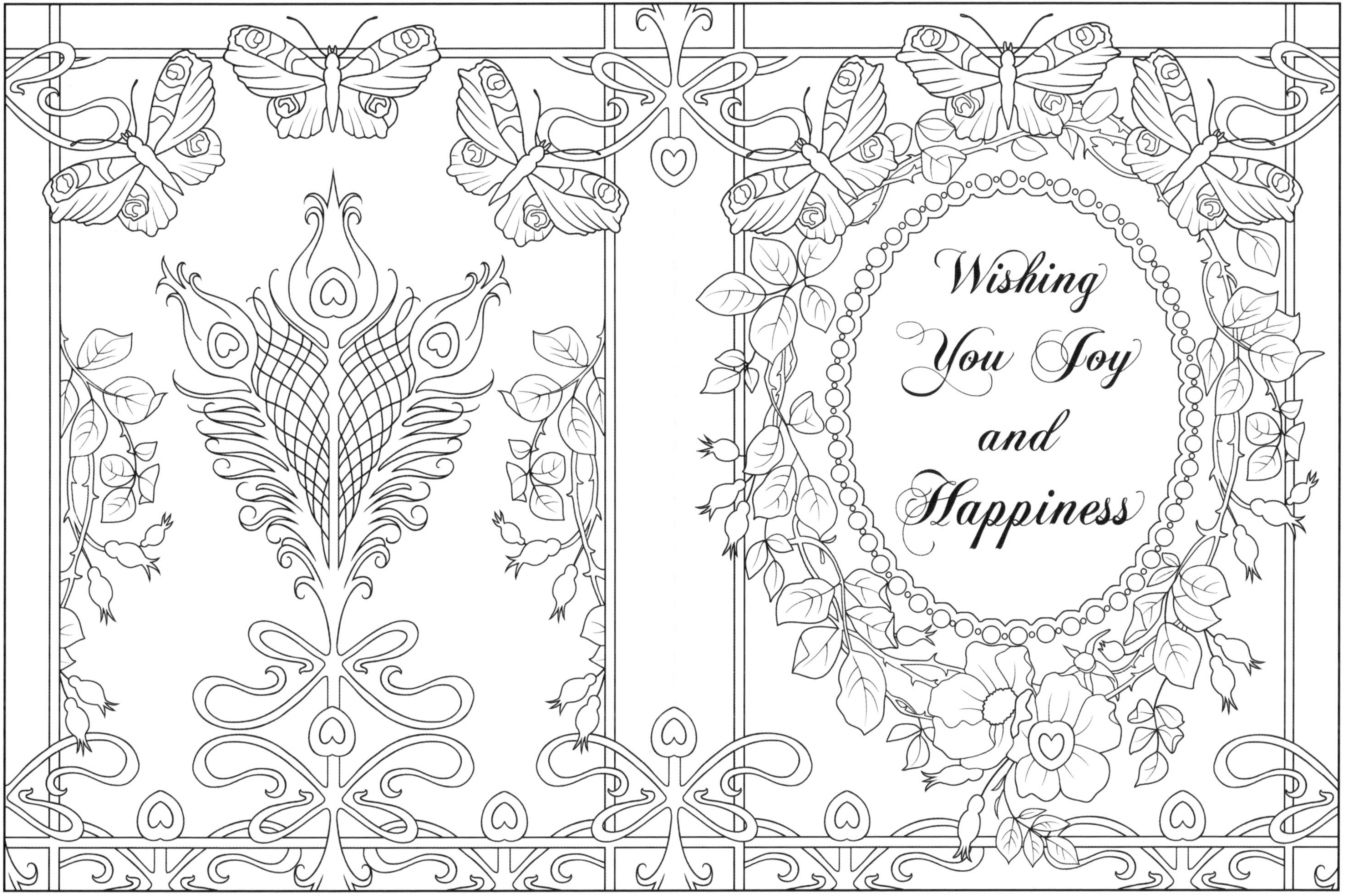
Wishing You Joy and Happiness

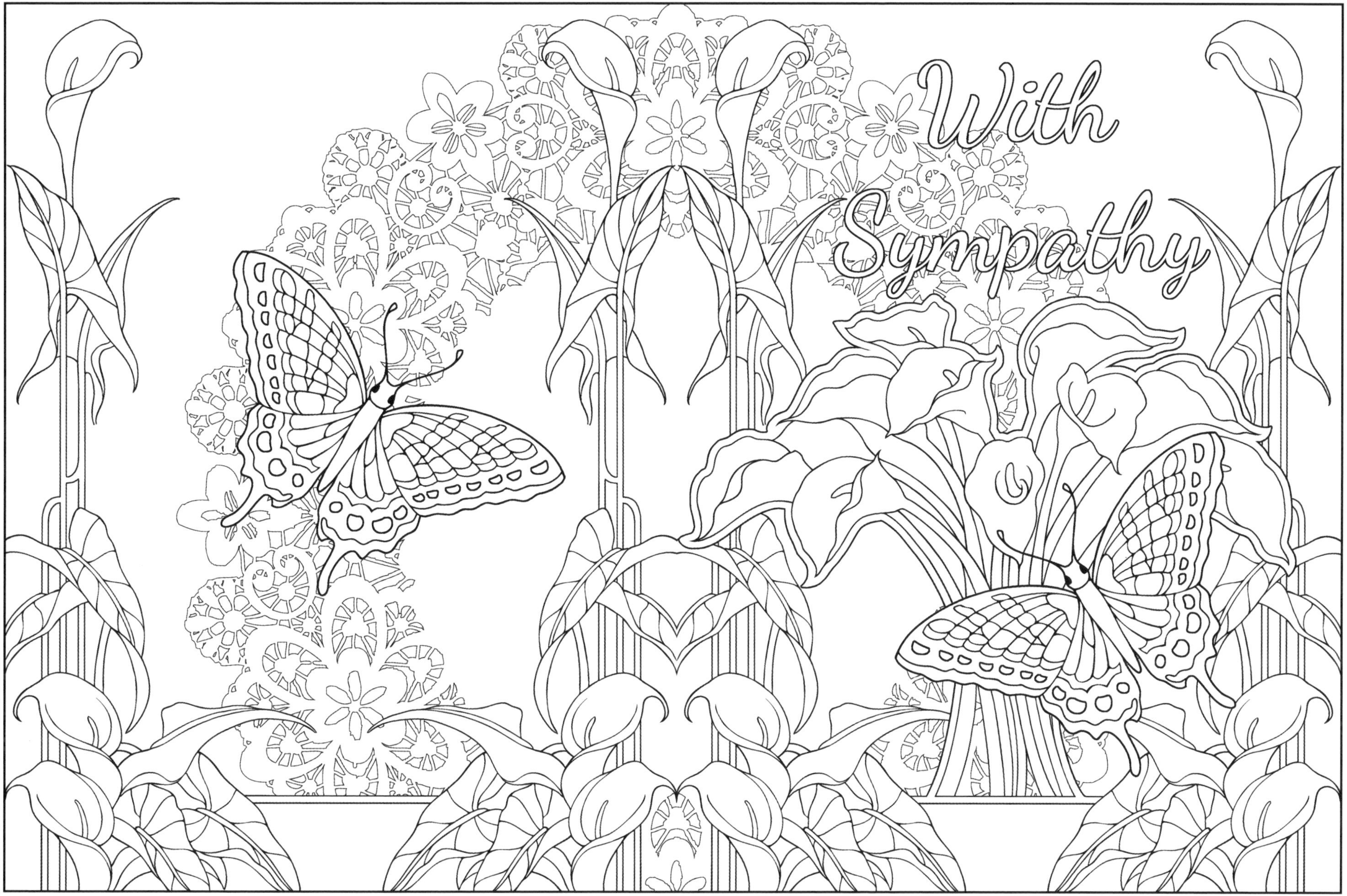
With Sympathy

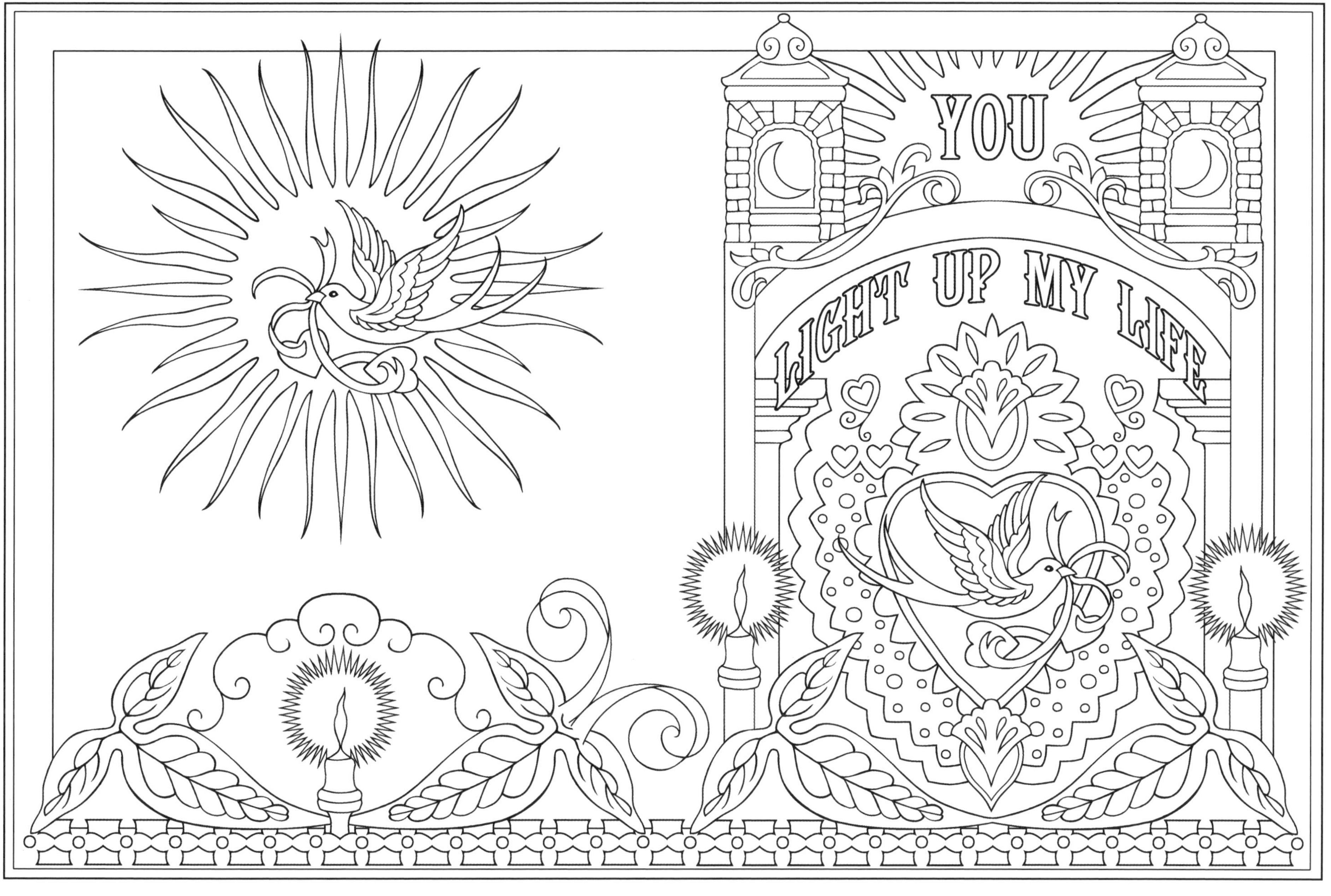
YOU
LIGHT UP MY LIFE

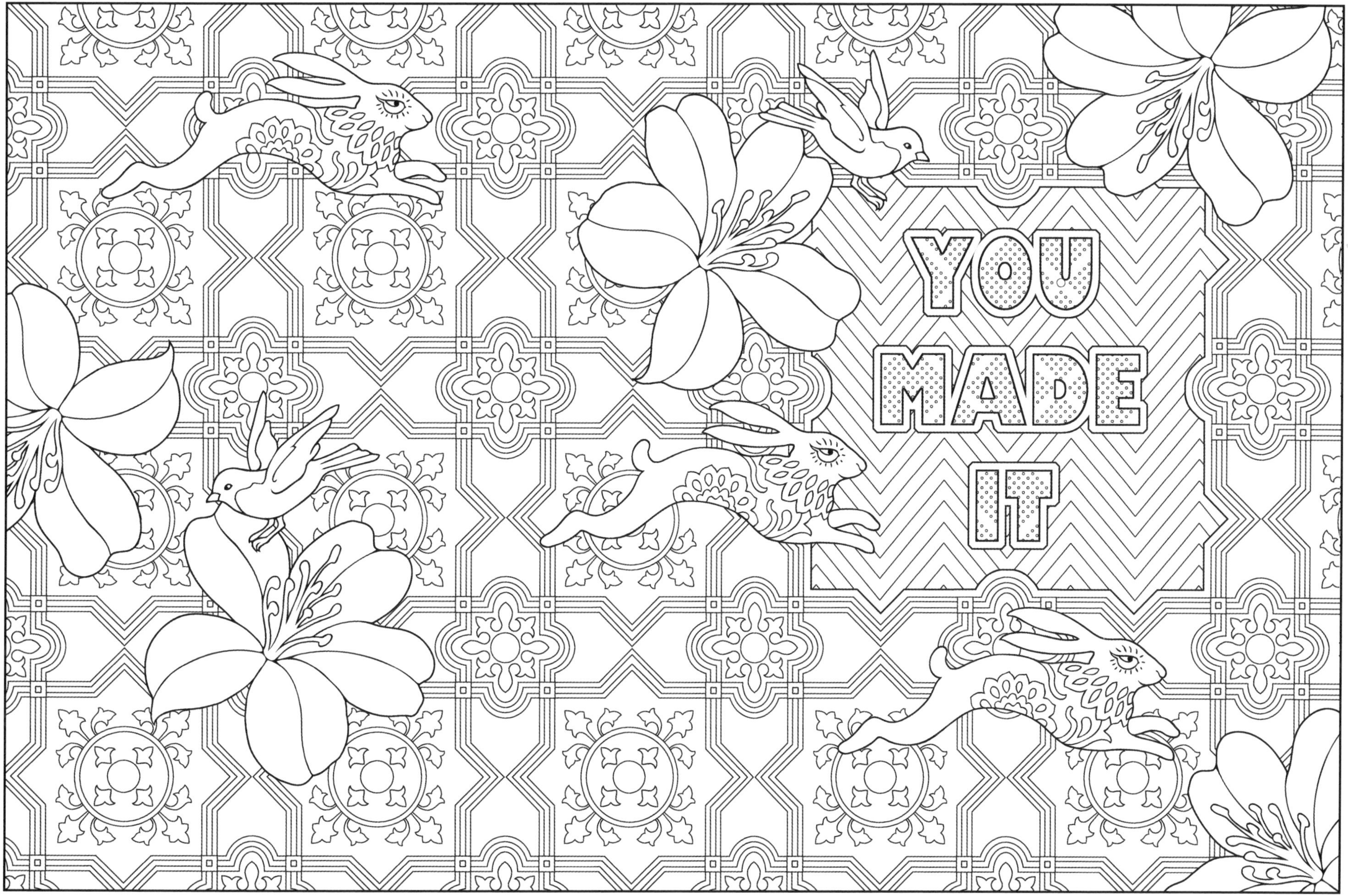
YOU
MADE
IT